nineteen, twenty

Hayley Grant

Presentation by *BookLeaf Publishing*

Web: www.bookleafpub.com

E-mail: info@bookleafpub.com

ISBN: 978-93-95755-99-3

First edition 2022

*For Mom, Dad and Jay, the receiving ends
of late night calls when everything was too
much*

four letter words

love taught me to sacrifice myself
hate taught me to love harder
pain taught me to find comfort in just about
anything
fear taught me to keep my mouth shut
and they all taught me that the weight of a word
can be so much more than the number of letters
it contains

sylvia

lips, a freshly washed apple
plump and glazed with deep red
old porcelain skin saw so much
but keeps a youthful glow
fingers dainty with tips of white
stacks upon stacks of gilt garnish
every curve and edge came from a blueprint
placed delicately by its creator
harmful and deadly seduction
to those who must never be seduced
such a thing from a horror novel
so brilliantly imagined but out of reach
only to be touched by something fictional
my mind grazes its soft hands over you
sylvia
but i must never tell a soul

objectify

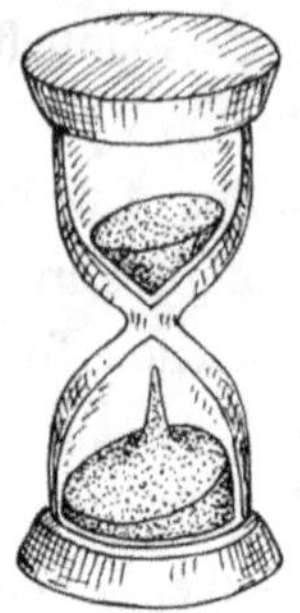

do i have a body or am i a body?
am i just a vessel containing this personality?
am i solely a control room for this fleshy thing i
call mine?
am i a piece of real estate waiting to become
home to the right person?
am i an object to be used?
or discarded following the rise of minimalism?
maybe i am one of a kind, a collectors item
maybe i am mass produced
when the updated version comes along will i be
useless to you?
will you just settle for me when you can't afford
my superior?
or will you see the charm in something vintage
like the love you've carried for ages?

when you're sleeping

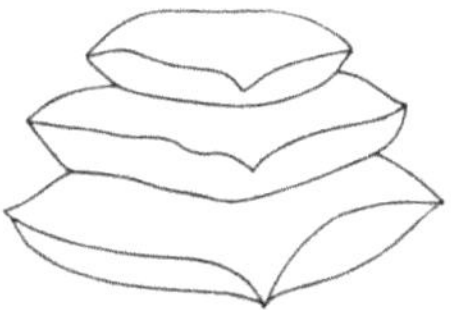

i used to admire your soft features
and slow breath
now i just feel alone and resentful
of the peace you're able to be at
while i'm wailing next to you

it's like nothing comes out when i scream
but my vocal cords work so well
better than your sense of hearing me ever will
your ears are there willing and ready
but your lack of empathy puts up a brick wall

when you're sleeping i lose feelings one by one
it's easier to leave someone who isn't aware
it's easier to be long gone before you wake up
i walk away with thousands of scars
and you lay there with not a single nightmare

i think i love her

you changed me in a way i never thought
getting to know her was more important than
any date we went on
obsessively looking for any clue that she was
still here
pulling her spirit out of thin air
mentioning things i knew about her to see if
your eyes lit up

i think i love her
and i need to make sure you don't
cause i so easily fell victim to her sky blue eyes
and i know not too long ago she cast a spell over
you too

anxious attachment

i didn't know i wanted it until
i became anxious for every time you called
i didn't know i needed it until
i became anxious every time you didn't
and i didn't know i needed to run until
i became anxious before you even left

identity crisis

i remember when i was younger
i think i was about fourteen
i kept seeing my friends getting into horrible
relationships
with horrible guys who hurt them
or cheated on them and manipulated them
i stood back on the sidelines
and watched them get crushed time and time
again
by the boys they placed high on a pedestal

back when i was younger
i didn't have much experience with love
the love of my family was the closest i had
gotten
so i looked at my friend
and i told myself i would never be that stupid
to love a guy that couldn't do the same

now i'm twenty
some would argue still young
but i look around and see myself living on my
own
feeding myself, working for myself
i must be some sort of mature

but no matter how mature i don't know who i am
this is an identity crisis
because i'm giving my all
to a man who's giving me nothing
and i sit alone at night crying
helplessly screaming for his love
like that'll do anything

i know so much
but i like to pretend i don't
self awareness hits me like a truck
when i least expect it
i'm asking myself why i let her down
that girl that told herself she wouldn't do

exactly what it is i'm doing

and part of the crisis comes from
not knowing whether i've grown
or lost the knowledge that i once carried so
proudly
all those years of school taught me the difference
between
there, their, and they're
but they forgot to tell me if its worth it
to give him the love of a mother
but be treated like a slave

back and forth

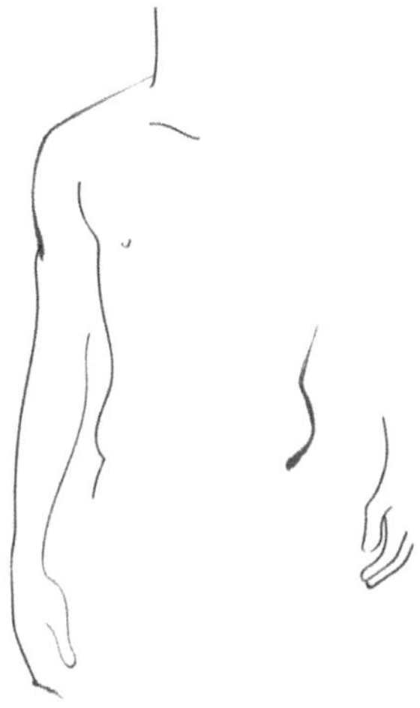

always back and forth between feelings of guilt
and anger
i left
but you made me

always back and forth between feeling safe and
scared
anger taught me security
but i knew deep down you were capable of much
more

always back and forth between wanting to be
with you or wanting to be free
but there wasn't an option for a little bit of both
and i needed there to be

always back and forth between feeling alone or
feeling lonely
because you either weren't physically there
or weren't really there

dissociate

dissociation
it feels like a dream
like you're not actually being beaten
the fist impacts your ability to feel
more than it impacts your flesh
my dissociation is protection
until they're done with you
and you lay there in blood and sweat
wishing they would've beat all the pain out of
you
just a little harder
and i would feel more bliss than guilt
all the things i must've done
for a person to stand over their finished job
and be proud of the damage they caused

the definition of opposite

i wonder how poor my vision must be that it
blurs the good with the bad
when growing up i was told they were opposites
but opposites attract
and that's what happened with you and me

now i look back and the opposites seem to not fit
the definition
cause they're more similar than not
like the passion in a screaming voice
and a scar in the shape of a heart

everything seems comfortable on the inside
looking out
cause the opposite i find most truly fits the
definition
is the difference between having you close
and not having you at all

epiphany

it took so long to find the nerve
then i so suddenly discovered being free

i wish i never met you but if i didn't

we wouldn't have gone on that trip to the zoo
we wouldn't have all of those inside jokes
we wouldn't have known what true love felt like
but we also wouldn't have
murdered each other's happiness time and time
again
and most importantly
these four walls wouldn't hold any unbearable
memories

ice cream date

april is coming to an end
spring fever hit a little harder this year
they opened an ice cream shop
just down the road from that building
that building where we found our first apartment
that building where we found ourselves laughing
and crying
and creating a life
or whatever you call struggling to buy furniture
a space filled by two kids

kids like ice cream and i sure did
i still do
and you know that
i hope you know that
i hope you think about the way my face would
light up when you walked back to the car with a

huge rainbow-sprinkled vanilla cone in your
hand
i hope you think about what it would be like to
experience that one more time
cause i do

when i saw that ice cream shop
the one just down the road from home
i saw you
i saw you walking back to the car with my huge
rainbow-sprinkled vanilla cone
i saw love

and you know
it's kinda funny
how vivid that image was
it's kinda funny
how vivid love can be
especially in our case
just two kids
two kids who love ice cream and loved each
other just as much

and you know
it's kinda funny
how you loved me
you loved me through bruises and scars and
tears
maybe you didn't know better

i mean, we were so young

and you know
it's kinda funny
how i loved you
maybe i found peace in my pain
peace in the thought that your touch was just as
vicious as the love you felt for me

and now april is coming to an end
and this kid didn't get her ice cream date
and you know
it's kinda funny
because now i'm feeling peace in the security of
not having you around
and i never thought i'd be able to feel this way
but i've realized that i'm not that innocent kid
anymore

and you know
it's kinda funny
because i've also realized that you never were

this is how you made me feel

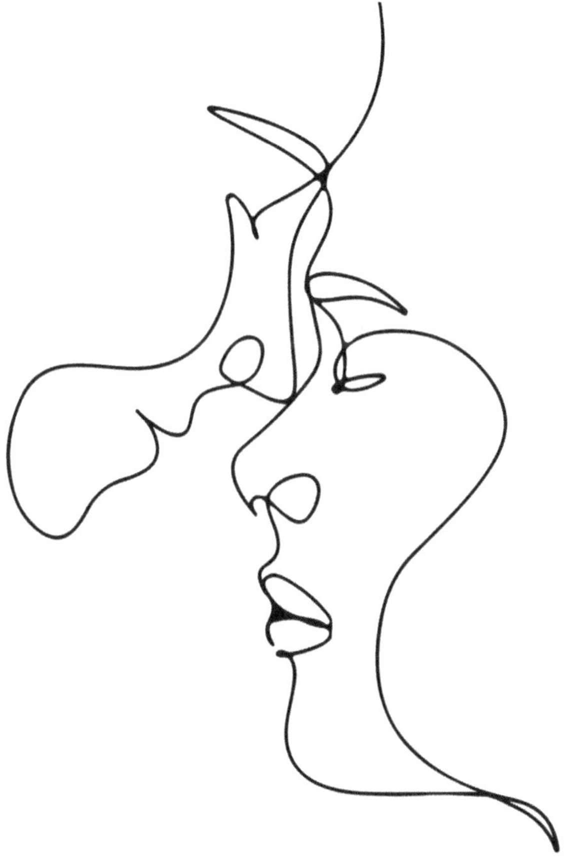

i stretched myself so very thin
that i couldn't stretch anymore
so i sprung right back together again
you pulled on me too hard but you didn't know

and i snapped
and all that was left of me was a useless piece of
rubber

you told me you wanted a normal elastic
or the nice one that you had lost before i came
around
or just one that you could make use of
but i wasn't able to fix myself the way you
wanted anymore
and you asked why
but i couldn't tell you that it was you who caused
the damage
because you wouldn't understand
or if you did
you would pretend not to
either way
i knew you'd snap too
and what good could come of two broken elastic
bands

no matter how useless i was
my philosophy was that if i kept you like new
i would never truly be useless at all

but then my rubber began to wear thin, fray and
crack
and i knew if i stayed any longer
i would not survive

the journey

finding yourself after leaving a long term partner
is
going to the grocery store and trying not to feel
sick
washing the dishes and trying not to feel empty
sleeping in your bed and trying not to feel cold
listening to music and trying not to play their
song
seeing a something funny and trying not to send
it to them
smiling and trying not to feel guilty
but mostly sitting all alone and trying not to get
consumed by your own thoughts

lively

dance like nobody's watching
no
i want you to watch me
i want you to take it all in
absorb the euphoria spilling out of me
with every movement and motion
appreciate what it takes to show this much
passion
reach out and touch me
feel the electric current running through your
fingertips
into the deepest part of your bones
join me
spin me around and i'll do the same for you
let's sink into each other
be lively until you run out of stamina
and we'll die together
when the lights come on

falling into love

i wake up in the night after dreaming
falling through the dark abyss
no perception of the ground below
weightless body, heavy with fear

i wake up in the night after dreaming
only to realize it wasn't a dream at all
i truly am falling into something unknown
entangled in a melancholy blanket of intimacy

autumnal

i wear his jacket
it doesn't keep me warm

August is for endings
hoping i'm able to get up
from the spot i've been sitting
all this time
but i've been trying

is the power of August
really powerful enough

or has it been lying to me
all this time
like so many things i'm used to

do i even know the truth
or am i living an autumnal lie?

nineteen,

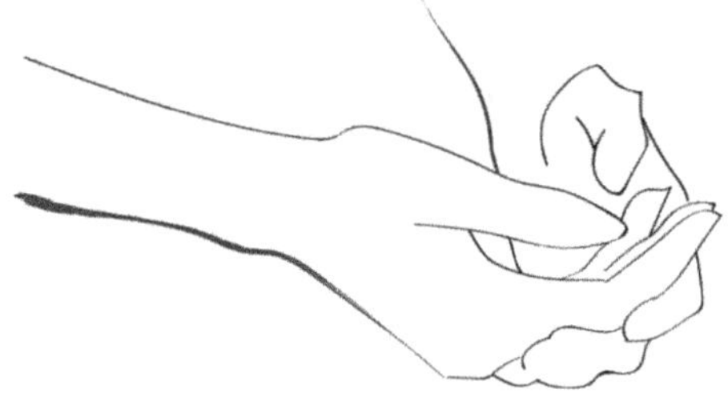

i was never that girl who partied
and had a huge friend group
and a fancy apartment
and an attractive boyfriend
until i was

there might be some truth in the phrase fake it til
you make it
but no one actually knew
i was lying about it all
i was in so deep

that even i didn't know

that partying was poisoning
and your friends hand-picked you cause they
thought you'd make them look better
and marble countertops were stone cold
and he didn't really care about you at all
there's nothing romantic about being an empty
alcoholic with no one to turn to

and that's what i learned at nineteen

twenty

being one with yourself isn't something i felt
until twenty
i realize a hobby isn't a way to distract yourself
from intrusive thoughts
you must immerse yourself in them
let them consume you
consume them
take all of the pain that you feel and spit it back
out
on a piece of paper
or a canvas
and call it fucking art

i'll always love you.

to my high school boyfriend
and my first year roommates
my childhood best friends
and my second love
the therapist who i only talked to once
and the one i've talked to tens of times
all of the boys i've fell for
and all of the girls too

i'll always love you

anyone who's ever crossed my path
once or a million times
you're in my heart
and there to stay

i'm one with nostalgia
i don't let go easy
if we've ever laughed
or looked up at the stars
know i have a song that reminds me of you

and no matter how it ended i look back on the
time and feel warm
because nineteen, twenty,
all the years before
and all the years to come
i lived

and to me, my blood, my breath, my skin
i'll always love you.

www.ingramcontent.com/pod-product-compliance
Lightning Source LLC
Chambersburg PA
CBHW061321140726
47998CB00006B/2500